slim & trim
recipes

Published by:
TRIDENT REFERENCE PUBLISHING
801 12th Avenue South, Suite 400
Naples, Fl 34102 USA

Tel: + 1 (239) 649-7077
www.tridentreference.com
email: sales@tridentreference.com

slim & trim

recipes

Publisher
Simon St. John Bailey

Editor-in-chief
Susan Knightley

Prepress
Precision Prep & Press

Includes Index
ISBN 1582797307
UPC 6 15269 97307 3

Printed in The United States

introduction

For too long weight loss methods have focused on restricting enjoyable food. Now we know the secret of sticking to a slimming meal plan is to keep it interesting. If you are a health-conscious and gourmet slimmer, this is the perfect book for you. Packed with creative recipes that everyone will love to eat, new ways to add flavor without adding calories and useful cooking tips, it has been thought for those who want to watch their

waistline and enjoy their favorite dishes at the same time.

Good food is truly one of life's great pleasures, and today many people look for a sensible approach to losing weight and staying slim. Here you will find great taste as well as great inspiration for healthy eating –and you will see at a glance the kilojoule/calorie content. Simply selecting different types of food relieves the problem of monotony. Our suggestions will show you how appetizing slimming food can be. They require no special ingredients and you may be surprised at the variety included. Not only are they good for you and your waistline, they are also delicious, quick and easy to prepare, and suitable for all the family.

This book will help you in the road to a slimmer, healthier body. It brings you light desserts that will satisfy any cravings for something sweet, and a number of mouthwatering recipes that will keep you looking good and feeling better.

Our guilt-free delights are so tempting no one will ever know they came from a slimming book –unless you tell them!

The Ideal Diet for You

- Is nutritionally balanced including a variety of foods.
- Is moderate in energy –about 1500 calories a day.
- Allows a weight loss of 1/2-1 kg/1-2 lb per week.
- Is flexible and fits in with your lifestyle and family.
- Can be followed for long periods of time.
- Uses ordinary foods and does not require special diet foods exclusively.

Ten Points to Break Bad Eating Habits

- Chew slowly.
- Sit down to eat.
- Use a small plate.
- Do nothing else while eating.
- Remove leftovers straight away.
- Don't skip meals.
- Don't nibble while cooking.
- Keep food out of sight.
- Keep busy.
- Stop negative thinking.

Difficulty scale

■☐☐ I Easy to do

■■☐ I Requires attention

■■■ I Requires experience

breakfast
in a cup

■□□ | Cooking time: 7 minutes - Preparation time: 10 minutes

ingredients

> 1 cup/250 ml/8 fl oz low fat milk
> $^1/_3$ cup/60 g/2 oz diet fruit yogurt
> 125 g/4 oz strawberries, hulled
> 1 tablespoon wheat germ
> 4 ice cubes

fruit and yogurt porridge

> 1 cup/250 ml/8 fl oz low fat milk
> $^1/_4$ cup/30 g/1 oz rolled oats
> 1$^1/_2$ tablespoons chopped dried apples
> 1$^1/_2$ tablespoons sultanas
> $^1/_2$ teaspoon ground cinnamon
> 1 tablespoon low fat natural yogurt

method

1. To make porridge, place milk, rolled oats, apples, sultanas and cinnamon in a saucepan and mix to combine. Cook over a medium heat, stirring, for 5-7 minutes or until oats are soft. Spoon porridge into serving bowls and serve topped with a spoonful of yogurt.

2. Place milk, yogurt, strawberries, wheat germ and ice in a food processor or blender and process until thick and frothy. Pour into a tall glass and serve immediately.

....
Serves 1

Glass: 1065 kilojoules/254 calories per serving
Porridge: 800 kilojoules/191 calories per serving

tip from the chef

Porridge is easy to make in the microwave. Place ingredients in a large microwavable container and cook on High (100%), stirring every 1$^1/_2$ minutes, for 3-4 minutes or until mixture boils and thickens.

pancake
sandwiches

■□□ | Cooking time: 25 minutes - Preparation time: 15 minutes

method

1 Combine flour and sugar in a bowl. Make a well in center of flour mixture, add egg and milk and mix until smooth.
2 Heat a nonstick frying pan over a medium heat, drop in tablespoons of batter and cook for 1 minute each side or until golden. Remove pancake, set aside and keep warm. Repeat with remaining batter to make 12 pancakes.
3 To make filling, place ricotta cheese, lemon juice and sugar in a food processor or blender and process until smooth.
4 To assemble, top half the pancakes with filling, then with remaining pancakes.
5 To make thickshake, place milk, fromage frais, chocolate topping or sauce and ice in a food processor or blender and process until thick and frothy. Pour into tall glasses and serve immediately.

ingredients

> $3/4$ cup/90 g/3 oz self-raising flour
> 1 tablespoon sugar
> 1 egg, lightly beaten
> $3/4$ cup/185 ml/6 fl oz low fat milk or buttermilk

lemon ricotta filling

> $1/2$ cup/125 g/4 oz low fat ricotta cheese
> 2 tablespoons lemon juice
> 1 tablespoon sugar

chocolate thickshake

> 2 cups/500 ml/16 fl oz low fat milk
> 200 g/$6^1/2$ oz low fat vanilla fromage frais
> 2 tablespoons low calorie chocolate topping or sauce
> 4 ice cubes

....
Serves 3

Pancakes: 569 kilojoules/136 calories per serving
Thickshake: 1313 kilojoules/313 calories per serving

tip from the chef

Pancakes can be made in advance and frozen, then reheated in the microwave when required. When freezing pancakes, place a piece of greaseproof paper between each one –this makes them easier to separate when you want to use them.

sweet
potato muffins

■□□ | Cooking time: 50 minutes - Preparation time: 15 minutes

ingredients

> **375 g/12 oz sweet potato, chopped**
> **1/2 cup/75 g/2^1/2 oz wholemeal self-raising flour**
> **1 cup/125 g/4 oz self-raising flour**
> **1/3 cup/60 g/2 oz brown sugar**
> **1 cup/200 g/6^1/2 oz low fat natural yogurt**
> **2 eggs, lightly beaten**
> **1 teaspoon vanilla essence**
> **3 tablespoons currants**
> **1 teaspoon ground cinnamon**

frozen smoothie

> **1 large banana, chopped and frozen**
> **2^1/2 cups/600 ml/1 pt ice-cold low fat milk**
> **3 tablespoons diet fruit yogurt**
> **4 ice cubes**

method

1. Boil or microwave sweet potato until tender, drain well and mash (a). Set aside to cool.
2. Place wholemeal flour, self-raising flour and sugar in a bowl and mix to combine. Make a well in center of flour mixture. Add yogurt, eggs, vanilla essence, currants and cinnamon and mix (b) until just combined. Fold sweet potato into flour mixture.
3. Spoon mixture into 12 greased 1/2 cup/ 125 ml/4 fl oz capacity muffin tins (c) and bake at 190°C/375°F/Gas 5 for 35 minutes or until muffins are cooked when tested with a skewer.
4. To make smoothie, place banana, milk, yogurt and ice cubes in a food processor or blender and process until thick and frothy. Pour into tall glasses and serve immediately.

Makes 12 muffins and 2 smoothies

Muffins: 554 kilojoules/132 calories per unit
Smoothie: 1075 kilojoules/257 calories per serving

tip from the chef

Make muffins when you have time and freeze them to have on hand for quick snacks. If you take your lunch to work, simply take a muffin out of the freezer in the morning –by mid-morning or lunch time it will be thawed.
For a different smoothie,

replace the banana with 1 mango, peeled, chopped and frozen, or with 250 g/8 oz strawberries, hulled, halved and frozen.
Keep frozen pieces of fruit in the freezer so that you can make this delicious smoothie at a moment's notice.

a

b

c

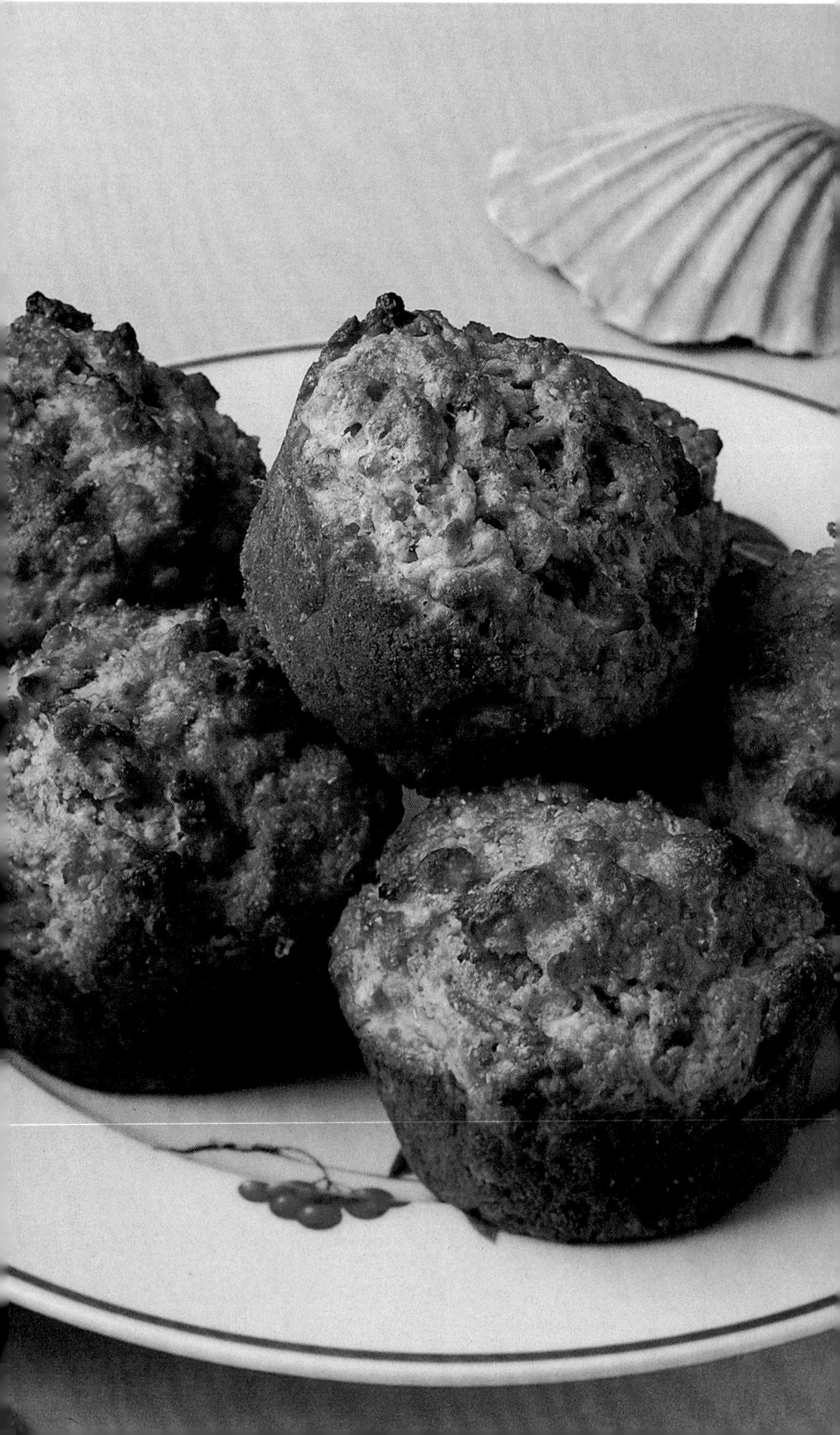

apple
and bran muffins

◾◻◻ | Cooking time: 15 minutes - Preparation time: 10 minutes

method

1. Sift together flour, nutmeg and baking powder into a bowl. Add bran cereal and sugar and mix to combine.
2. Make a well in center of flour mixture. Add apples, eggs, yogurt and oil and mix until just combined.
3. Spoon mixture into 12 greased 1/2 cup/ 125 ml/4 fl oz muffin tins and bake at 180°C/350°F/Gas 4 for 15 minutes or until muffins are cooked when tested with a skewer.

Makes 12

550 kilojoules/130 calories per unit

ingredients

> 1 1/2 cups/230 g/7 1/2 oz wholemeal self-raising flour
> 1/2 teaspoon ground nutmeg
> 1/4 teaspoon baking powder
> 1/2 cup/30 g/1 oz bran cereal, toasted
> 1/3 cup/60 g/2 oz brown sugar
> 2 green apples, grated
> 2 eggs, lightly beaten
> 1/4 cup/45 g/1 1/2 oz low fat natural yogurt
> 1 tablespoon polyunsaturated oil

tip from the chef

The secret to making great muffins is in the mixing –they should be mixed as little as possible, it doesn't matter if the mixture is lumpy. Overmixing the mixture will result in tough muffins.

quiche rolls

■□□ | Cooking time: 25 minutes - Preparation time: 15 minutes

ingredients

> **4 wholemeal rolls**

tuna filling

> **220 g/7 oz canned tuna in brine or springwater, drained and flaked**
> **60 g/2 oz canned sweet corn kernels, drained**
> **30 g/1 oz reduced fat Cheddar cheese, grated**
> **1/2 cup/125 ml/4 fl oz low fat milk**
> **2 eggs, lightly beaten**
> **2 tablespoons snipped fresh chives**
> **freshly ground black pepper**

method

1. Cut tops from rolls and scoop out center of roll to make a thin shell. Place shells on a baking tray and set aside. Reserve tops and bread from center of rolls for another use.

2. To make filling, place tuna, sweet corn, cheese, milk, eggs, chives and black pepper to taste in a bowl and mix to combine.

3. Carefully pour filling into rolls and bake at 180°C/350°F/Gas 4 for 25 minutes or until filling is set. Serve hot, warm or cold.

....
Serves 4

1718 kilojoules/411 calories per unit

tip from the chef

The bread from the center of the rolls can be made into breadcrumbs.
Salmon makes a tasty alternative to the tuna in this recipe.

crispy pizza rolls

■□□ | Cooking time: 20 minutes - Preparation time: 15 minutes

method

1 Spread each bread round with 1 tablespoon tomato paste (purée) leaving a 2 cm/3/4 in border. Sprinkle with green pepper, ham, spring onions and cheese.

2 Roll up bread rounds and cut in half. Secure with a wooden toothpick or cocktail stick.

3 Place rolls on baking trays and bake at 180°C/350°F/Gas 4 for 20 minutes or until bread is crisp. Serve hot or cold.

ingredients

> **2 large wholemeal pitta bread rounds, split**
> **4 tablespoons tomato paste (purée)**
> **1/2 green pepper, chopped**
> **2 slices reduced fat ham, chopped**
> **2 spring onions, chopped**
> **60 g/2 oz reduced fat Cheddar cheese, grated**

....
Makes 8

428 kilojoules/102 calories per unit

tip from the chef

For a vegetarian version of this snack simply omit the ham. Baked beans, artichoke hearts, avocado or fresh mushrooms can be used instead, if you wish.

florentine
egg rounds

■ ■ □ | Cooking time: 20 minutes - Preparation time: 10 minutes

method

Blanch spinach leaves in boiling water or in the microwave on High (100%) for 10 seconds or until they just change color. Drain and pat dry on absorbent kitchen paper.

Line two 1 cup/250 ml/8 fl oz capacity ramekins with spinach. Divide red pepper between ramekins. Break an egg into a cup or small jug, then gently pour into one ramekin. Repeat with remaining egg.

Place ramekins in a baking dish with enough hot water to come halfway up the sides of the ramekins and bake at 180°C/350°F/Gas 4 for 15-20 minutes or until eggs are cooked to your liking.

To make sauce, place mayonnaise, yogurt, parsley, mustard and black pepper to taste in a bowl and mix to combine.

To serve, run a knife around the edge of the ramekins and unmold. Place egg rounds on muffins, accompany with sauce and serve.

ingredients

> **4 spinach leaves**
> **1/2 red pepper, diced**
> **2 eggs**
> **2 wholemeal or mixed grain muffins, split and toasted**

mustard sauce

> **2 tablespoons light mayonnaise**
> **1 tablespoon low fat natural yogurt**
> **2 teaspoons chopped fresh parsley**
> **1/2 teaspoon wholegrain mustard**
> **freshly ground black pepper**

....
Serves 2

1277 kilojoules/305 calories per serving

tip from the chef

Lunch is the meal most often missed. It is, however, the pitstop most needed to get you through the daily work at the office or at home. It also stops the snack attack which, if one succumbs, can result in a diet blow-out. Recipes like this one will help you not to miss lunch.

pumpkin soufflé

■□□ | Cooking time: 30 minutes - Preparation time: 15 minutes

ingredients

- > **1 tablespoon butter**
- > **2 tablespoons flour**
- > **1¹/₂ cups skim milk**
- > **4 eggs, separated**
- > **1³/₄ cups canned pumpkin**
- > **freshly ground black pepper**

method

1. Melt butter in a saucepan. Stir in flour and cook for 1 minute. Gradually mix in milk (a). Cook until sauce boils and thickens. Remove pan from heat.

2. Beat egg yolks into white sauce and mix in canned pumpkin (b). Season with black pepper to taste.

3. Beat egg whites until stiff peaks form and fold into pumpkin mixture (c).

4. Divide mixture between four 1¹/₂ cups capacity individual soufflé dishes. Bake in a preheated oven at 200°C/400°F/Gas 6 for 20-25 minutes, or until soufflés are puffed and golden. Serve immediately.

....
Serves 4

879 kilojoules/210 calories per serving

tip from the chef

If you choose this easy dish for a vegetarian dinner party, remember that a platter of crisp raw vegetables is a good way to start off the meal. Guests can nibble on them or dunk into a dip in place of crackers. They are light and refreshing and won't spoil your appetite for the main course.

a

b

c

cheesy vegetable strudel

■□□ | Cooking time: 35 minutes - Preparation time: 15 minutes

method

1. To make filling, heat oil in a frying pan. Cook onion and garlic for 2-3 minutes. Add mushrooms and cook for 3-4 minutes. Shake as much water as possible from spinach and add to pan. Cook until spinach starts to wilt.

2. Squeeze spinach mixture to remove excess liquid. Combine with cheeses and egg, season with black pepper to taste.

3. Layer two sheets of filo pastry. Brush top sheet very lightly with oil, top with remaining two sheets and brush with oil.

4. Spread filling over pastry leaving about 2.5 cm/1 in border. Fold in sides of pastry and roll up from the longest side. Place roll on a baking tray and brush lightly with oil. Sprinkle with sesame seeds.

5. Bake at 200°C/400°F/Gas 6 for 20-25 minutes, or until golden.

ingredients

> 4 sheets filo pastry
> 2 tablespoons olive oil
> 2 tablespoons sesame seeds

filling

> 2 teaspoons olive oil
> 1 onion, chopped
> 1 clove garlic, crushed
> 150 g/5 oz mushrooms, sliced
> 1 bunch spinach (about 1 kg/2 lb), washed
> 1 cup cottage cheese
> 3/4 cup crumbled feta cheese
> 1 egg
> freshly ground black pepper

Serves 6

850 kilojoules/203 calories per serving

tip from the chef

When trying recipes like these, which are higher in fat and sodium, balance out the rest of your meals for the day with less fat and salt. What you need is an overall, balanced nutritious food plan.

salmon
and lentil salad

■□□ | Cooking time: 5 minutes - Preparation time: 10 minutes

ingredients

> 1 cos lettuce, leaves separated and torn into large pieces
> 200 g/6$^1/_2$ oz green lentils, cooked and drained
> 200 g/6$^1/_2$ oz red lentils, cooked and drained
> 250 g/8 oz cherry tomatoes, halved
> 155 g/5 oz wholemeal croûtons
> 1 tablespoon polyunsaturated oil
> 375 g/12 oz salmon fillets, cut into 3 cm/ 1$^1/_4$ in wide strips
> fresh Parmesan cheese
> freshly ground black pepper

creamy dressing

> $^1/_2$ cup/125 ml/4 fl oz light mayonnaise
> 2 tablespoons vegetable stock
> 1 tablespoon wholegrain mustard
> 1 tablespoon white wine vinegar

method

1. To make dressing, place mayonnaise, stock, mustard and vinegar in a bowl and mix to combine. Set aside.

2. Arrange lettuce, lentils, tomatoes and croûtons attractively on a serving platter. Set aside.

3. Heat oil in a frying pan over a medium heat, add salmon and cook, turning several times, for 4 minutes or until cooked. Remove from pan and arrange on top of salad.

4. Drizzle dressing over salad and top with shavings of Parmesan cheese and black pepper to taste.

....

Serves 4

2511 kilojoules/600 calories per serving

tip from the chef

The iron content of legumes such as lentils is fairly high, but as it occurs in an inorganic form, the human body needs help to absorb it. You can increase the body's ability to absorb the iron if you serve a vitamin C-rich food (such as the salad here) as part of the same meal.

marinated
fish salad

■□□ | Cooking time: 0 minute - Preparation time: 10 minutes

method

Combine lemon juice, lime juice and coriander in a shallow glass or ceramic dish. Add fish, cover and refrigerate for 3-4 hours, turning occasionally.

To make dressing, place ginger, chili, garlic, oil and pepper in a screwtop jar and shake to combine.

Arrange lettuce leaves on serving platter. Drain fish and arrange on lettuce leaves. Pour dressing over and top with onion rings and orange segments.

Serves 4

879 kilojoules/210 calories per serving

ingredients

> 1 cup lemon juice
> 1 cup lime juice
> 4 tablespoons finely chopped fresh coriander
> 4 firm white fish fillets
> lettuce leaves
> 1 onion, sliced into rings
> 420 g/14 oz canned orange segments, drained

dressing

> 1 teaspoon grated fresh ginger
> 1 small fresh red chili, seeded and finely chopped
> 1 clove garlic, crushed
> 1 tablespoon polyunsaturated oil
> freshly ground black pepper

tip from the chef

You will find that the fish turns opaque after marinating in citrus juices, because of the acidity of the juices. Try to eat fish at least two times a week. Fish is an excellent food, high in protein, vitamins and minerals, but low in fat and cholesterol. Our marinated fish salad is ideal for weight watchers and cholesterol watchers alike.

spanish
garlic shrimp

■□□ | Cooking time: 20 minutes - Preparation time: 5 minutes

ingredients

- > 1 1/2 tablespoons butter
- > 1 tablespoon polyunsaturated oil
- > 8 cloves garlic, crushed
- > 6 green onions, chopped
- > 1 small red chili, seeded and chopped
- > 420 g/14 oz canned tomatoes, undrained and mashed
- > 1 kg/2 lb shrimp, shelled and deveined, with tails left intact

method

1. Heat butter and oil in a frying pan. Cook garlic, green onions and chili for 1-2 minutes. Stir in tomatoes and cook over medium heat until boiling.
2. Divide shrimp between 4 individual ovenproof dishes. Spoon tomato mixture over and bake at 200°C/400°F/Gas 6 for 10-15 minutes, or until shrimp turn pink.

....

Serves 4

1456 kilojoules/348 calories per serving

tip from the chef

A gourmet delight made lighter and healthier for today. Garlic shrimp are usually cooked and served in lots of butter and olive oil. To reduce fat, we cooked ours in just a little butter for taste plus 1 tablespoon oil.

cebiche
in witlof leaves

■ ■ □ | Cooking time: 0 minute - Preparation time: 20 minutes

method

1. Using a very sharp knife, cut fish into paper thin slices (this will be easier to do if you place the fish in the freezer for 10 minutes before slicing —take care not to allow the fish to freeze).

2. Divide fish between witlof leaves. Scatter each with some onion and a few capers.

3. To make dressing, place oil, lime juice, vinegar and horseradish relish in a small bowl and whisk to combine.

4. Drizzle dressing over fish. Serve immediately with crostini or fresh crusty bread.

....

Serves 6

513 kilojoules/123 calories per serving

ingredients

> **200 g very fresh tuna or swordfish fillets**
> **4 witlof, leaves separated**
> **1 red onion, diced**
> **1 tablespoon capers, rinsed and drained**

lime and horseradish dressing

> **2 tablespoons olive oil**
> **2 tablespoons lime juice**
> **1 tablespoon sherry or white wine vinegar**
> **1 teaspoon horseradish relish**

tip from the chef

Use only the freshest fish for this recipe —tell your fishmonger what you are using it for and they will advise you what will be appropriate.

chicken
and lima bean bake

■ ■ ☐ | Cooking time: 75 minutes - Preparation time: 15 minutes

ingredients

> 1 slice bacon, chopped
> 1 x 1 kg/2 lb chicken, cut into pieces, skin removed
> 2 onions, chopped
> 1 clove garlic, crushed
> 1/2 cup degreased chicken stock
> 4 tablespoons white wine
> 1 teaspoon mixed Italian herbs
> 1 teaspoon sugar
> 450 g/15 oz canned tomatoes, undrained and mashed
> 300 g/10 oz canned lima beans, drained

method

1. Place bacon in a frying pan and cook for 2-3 minutes or until crisp. Remove from pan and set aside.
2. Brown chicken pieces in bacon drippings; remove from pan. Add onions and garlic and cook for 2-3 minutes, until onions soften. Transfer chicken and onions mixture to an ovenproof dish.
3. Add stock, wine, herbs, sugar and tomatoes to pan and cook over medium heat until mixture boils and thickens, stirring occasionally. Add lima beans.
4. Sprinkle chicken with bacon and pour sauce over. Cover and bake at 200°C/400°F/Gas 6 for 1 hour, or until chicken is tender.

....
Serves 6

431 kilojoules/103 calories per serving

tip from the chef

We added flavor with onions, garlic, wine and herbs in tomato sauce. There is no need for salt when you can make imaginative use of fragrant ingredients.

spiced
apricot chicken

■□□ | Cooking time: 55 minutes - Preparation time: 10 minutes

method

1. Set aside 6 apricots. Place remaining apricots, reserved juice, chili, cumin, coriander, curry powder, turmeric, lemon rind and coconut milk in a food processor or blender and process until smooth.

2. Heat oil in a frying pan. Cook onions, garlic and ginger for 2-3 minutes. Add chicken pieces and brown well on each side.

3. Pour apricot purée over chicken and cook, uncovered, over low heat for 45-50 minutes or until chicken is tender.

4. Chop reserved apricots and combine with yogurt. Serve with chicken.

....
Serves 6

1535 kilojoules/366 calories per serving

ingredients

- > 750 g/1 1/2 lb unsweetened canned apricots, drained, juice reserved
- > 1 small red chili, seeded and finely chopped
- > 2 teaspoons ground cumin
- > 2 teaspoons ground coriander
- > 1/2 teaspoon curry powder
- > 1 teaspoon ground turmeric
- > 2 teaspoons grated lemon rind
- > 3 tablespoons coconut milk
- > 1 tablespoon polyunsaturated oil
- > 2 onions, chopped
- > 2 cloves garlic, crushed
- > 1 teaspoon grated fresh ginger
- > 1 x 1 kg/2 lb chicken, cut into pieces, skin removed
- > 250 g/8 oz low fat natural yogurt

tip from the chef

Avoid deep-frying and roasting in fat. Instead grill, dry-roast, stir-fry, microwave or braise meat and chicken. If meat requires browning, brush pan with oil (don't pour it in) and cook quickly over high heat to seal in juices.

spicy roast chicken

■□□ | Cooking time: 1 hour - Preparation time: 15 minutes

ingredients

> **1 x 1 kg/2 lb chicken, skin removed**
> **2 tablespoons honey**
> **2 teaspoons sesame seeds**

spice mixture

> **2 cloves garlic, crushed**
> **1 teaspoon grated fresh ginger**
> **2 teaspoons low salt soy sauce**
> **3 teaspoons curry powder**
> **1/2 teaspoon garam masala**
> **3 tablespoons lemon juice**

method

1. To make spice mixture, blend together garlic, ginger, soy sauce, curry powder, garam masala and lemon juice.
2. Place chicken on a roasting rack in a baking dish; rub with spice mixture. Bake at 180°C/350°F/Gas 4 for 45 minutes.
3. Warm honey and brush over chicken. Cook for 15 minutes longer. Sprinkle chicken with sesame seeds 5 minutes before cooking is completed.

....
Serves 6

2068 kilojoules/499 calories per serving

tip from the chef

To cook chicken in the microwave, arrange chicken, breast side down, in a microwave-safe dish. Cook on High (100%) for 15 minutes each side. Heat honey in a small microwave-safe dish on High (100%) for 30 seconds and pour over chicken. Sprinkle with sesame seeds and cook on High (100%) for 2 minutes. Stand, covered with foil, for 10 minutes before serving.

turkey caesar salad

method

1 Heat a nonstick frying pan over a medium heat. Add turkey and cook, stirring, for 4 minutes or until crisp. Drain on absorbent kitchen paper and set aside to cool.

2 Boil, steam or microwave asparagus until just tender. Drain and refresh under cold running water.

3 Arrange lettuce, asparagus, tomatoes and bread slices in a large serving bowl or on a platter. Scatter with turkey and top with Parmesan cheese shavings.

4 To make dressing, place mayonnaise, yogurt, mustard and black pepper to taste in a bowl and mix to combine.

5 Drizzle dressing over salad, cover and refrigerate until ready to serve.

....
Serves 4

ingredients

> 4 slices lean turkey breast, cut into strips
> 250 g/8 oz asparagus spears, blanched
> 1 cos lettuce, leaves separated
> 250 g/8 oz cherry tomatoes, halved
> 1 small French bread stick, sliced and toasted
> fresh Parmesan cheese

mustard yogurt dressing

> 2 tablespoons light mayonnaise
> 4 tablespoons low fat natural yogurt
> 2 teaspoons wholegrain mustard
> freshly ground black pepper

891 kilojoules/213 calories per serving

tip from the chef

To make shavings of Parmesan cheese you will need a piece of fresh Parmesan cheese. Use a vegetable peeler or a coarse grater to remove shavings from the cheese.

best-ever
hamburgers

■□□ | Cooking time: 10 minutes - Preparation time: 15 minutes

ingredients

> **750 g/1 1/2 lb lean beef mince**
> **1 onion, very finely chopped**
> **1 carrot, finely grated**
> **1 tablespoon Worcestershire sauce**
> **1 tablespoon ketchup**
> **dash chili sauce**
> **1/2 teaspoon dried oregano**
> **1/2 teaspoon dried thyme**
> **freshly ground black pepper**
> **6 wholemeal rolls, split**
> **lettuce leaves**
> **6 slices cooked beetroot**
> **6 slices cucumber**
> **2 tomatoes, sliced**

method

1. Combine beef mince, onion, carrot, Worcestershire sauce, ketchup, chili sauce, oregano, thyme and black pepper to taste in a large bowl and mix well.

2. Wet hands and shape mixture into 6 patties. Cook in a nonstick frying pan for 5-6 minutes, pressing down with a spatula.

3. To assemble burgers, toast rolls. Place lettuce, burger, beetroot, cucumber and tomato on bottom half of each roll. Top with remaining half roll.

....
Serves 6

1674 kilojoules/400 calories per serving

tip from the chef

Just because you are watching what you eat, there is no need to give up all the best things in life. These delicious hamburgers will satisfy all the family –and you needn't tell them just how healthy they are!

marinated
beef kebabs

◼☐☐ | Cooking time: 10 minutes - Preparation time: 15 minutes

method

1 Trim all visible fat from meat and cut into 2.5 cm/1 in cubes. Set aside.

2 To make marinade, combine yogurt, mustard, gherkins, garlic, sherry and black pepper to taste in a glass bowl. Add meat (a) and marinate for 1 hour.

3 Remove meat from marinade and thread onto 8 skewers, alternating with onions, mushrooms and peppers (b).

4 Grill kebabs (c) over medium heat for 8-10 minutes, turning and basting frequently with marinade. Serve kebabs with any remaining marinade as an accompaniment.

....
Serves 4

2049 kilojoules/488 calories per serving

ingredients

> **500 g/1 lb lean topside steak**
> **8 small onions**
> **120 g/4 oz button mushrooms**
> **1/2 red pepper, cubed**
> **1/2 green pepper, cubed**

marinade

> **3/4 cup low fat natural yogurt**
> **2 teaspoons wholegrain mustard**
> **1 tablespoon finely chopped gherkins**
> **1 clove garlic, crushed**
> **2 tablespoons dry sherry**
> **freshly ground black pepper**

tip from the chef

Taste your food before adding salt. Too many people automatically reach for the salt shaker without even tasting if the food is seasoned.

a

b

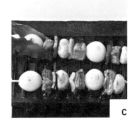
c

red
wine steaks

◼️◻️◻️ | Cooking time: 15 minutes - Preparation time: 10 minutes

ingredients

> **4 lean beef steaks**

red wine marinade

> 1/4 cup/60 ml/2 fl oz red wine
> 2 tablespoons Worcestershire sauce
> 2 teaspoons French mustard
> freshly ground black pepper

mixed mushroom sauté

> 155 g/5 oz button mushrooms
> 155 g/5 oz oyster mushrooms
> 125 g/4 oz flat mushrooms, sliced
> 1/2 cup/125 ml/4 fl oz dry white wine
> 2 teaspoons green peppercorns in brine, drained
> 1 tablespoon chopped fresh thyme or 1 teaspoon dried thyme

method

1. To make marinade, place wine, Worcestershire sauce, mustard and black pepper to taste in a shallow dish and mix to combine. Add steaks to marinade and set aside to marinate for at least 30 minutes.

2. Cook steaks on a preheated hot barbecue or under a grill for 3-5 minutes each side or until cooked to your liking.

3. To make sauté, heat a nonstick frying pan over a medium heat. Add button, oyster and flat mushrooms and cook, stirring, for 2-3 minutes. Stir in wine, green peppercorns and thyme and cook, stirring, for 5 minutes longer or until mushrooms are tender. Serve with steaks.

....
Serves 4

1298 kilojoules/310 calories per serving

tip from the chef

When testing to see if steaks are cooked to your liking, press with a pair of blunt tongs. Do not cut the meat. Rare steaks will feel springy to touch, medium steaks slightly springy and well-done steaks will feel firm.

beef
and mushroom pie

a

b

c

■ ■ ■ | Cooking time: 90 minutes - Preparation time: 20 minutes

method

1. Cut meat into 2.5 cm/1 in cubes. Set aside.
2. Heat 1 tablespoon oil in a large saucepan and cook onion and mushrooms for 2-3 minutes. Add meat and stock. Season to taste with black pepper. Bring to the boil, then reduce heat and simmer for 40-50 minutes, or until meat is tender. Return to boiling. Whisk in cornflour mixture, stirring until sauce thickens. Cool.
3. Layer pastry sheets on top of each other, brushing between layers with remaining oil (a). Place a 22 cm/9 in pie plate upside down on pastry and cut a circle 2.5 cm/1 in larger than dish through all the layers of pastry.
4. Line pie plate with 8 pastry circles. Spread filling over pastry (b) and top with remaining 4 pastry circles. Roll down edges of pastry (c) and brush top with oil. Sprinkle with poppy seeds. Bake at 180°C/350°F/Gas 4 for 30 minutes, or until golden brown.

ingredients

> **500 g/1 lb lean topside steak, trimmed of visible fat**
> **4 tablespoons polyunsaturated oil**
> **1 onion, chopped**
> **120 g/4 oz mushrooms, sliced**
> **1¼ cups beef stock**
> **freshly ground black pepper**
> **2 tablespoons cornflour blended with 4 tablespoons water**
> **12 sheets filo pastry**
> **1 tablespoon poppy seeds**

....
Serves 6

856 kilojoules/214 calories per serving

tip from the chef

Instead of the traditional shortcrust or puff pastry, we have used sheets of fine filo pastry brushed sparingly with oil. Not only is the fat content reduced, but the pastry is crisp and light, never soggy. Lean beef has been selected for the filling and cooked with vegetables for extra flavor and fiber. The pie ends up being modest in fat, salt and calories –a satisfying, yet healthy, dish that everyone can enjoy.

peppered
lamb cutlets

■ □ □ | Cooking time: 10 minutes - Preparation time: 10 minutes

ingredients
- > **8 lean lamb cutlets**
- > **2 tablespoons French mustard**
- > **2 tablespoons cracked black peppercorns**
- > **1 tablespoon polyunsaturated oil**
- > **2 teaspoons brandy**
- > **1 teaspoon Worcestershire sauce**
- > **1 tablespoon evaporated skim milk**
- > **2 teaspoons snipped fresh chives**

method
1. Trim meat of visible fat. Spread mustard over each side of cutlets; press on peppercorns. Heat oil in a frying pan and cook cutlets for 4-5 minutes on each side. Remove cutlets to serving platter and keep warm.
2. Combine brandy, Worcestershire sauce, skim milk and chives. Stir into juices in pan. Heat quickly, stirring constantly to lift browned bits from bottom of pan. Spoon sauce over cutlets and serve.

....
Serves 4

2155 kilojoules/515 calories per serving

tip from the chef

With today's leaner cuts of meat, you can still enjoy a tasty juicy cutlet, but remember to keep meat portions moderate. About 125 g/¹/₄ lb meat per person is sufficient to supply al necessary iron, protein and B vitamins.

pork satays
with peanut sauce

■□□ | Cooking time: 15 minutes - Preparation time: 15 minutes

method

1. To make marinade, combine all ingredients in a large glass bowl. Add meat and marinate for 30 minutes.

2. To make sauce, heat oil in a saucepan, cook onion and garlic for 1 minute. Stir in curry powder, peanut butter, soy sauce, chili sauce, water and lemon juice. Bring to the boil, reduce heat and simmer, uncovered, for 5 minutes or until sauce thickens. Set aside.

3. Remove meat from marinade and thread onto 8 skewers; reserve marinade. Grill over medium heat for 8-10 minutes, turning and basting frequently with marinade. Serve with sauce.

....
Serves 4

1205 kilojoules/287 calories per serving

ingredients

> **500 g/1 lb lean pork, cubed**

marinade

> **2 tablespoons low salt soy sauce**
> **2 tablespoons lemon juice**
> **1 tablespoon brown sugar**
> **2 cloves garlic, crushed**
> **1/2 teaspoon ground coriander**
> **1/4 teaspoon ground cumin**
> **1/2 teaspoon grated fresh ginger**
> **freshly ground black pepper**

peanut sauce

> **1 tablespoon polyunsaturated oil**
> **1 onion, finely chopped**
> **2 cloves garlic, crushed**
> **1 1/2 teaspoons curry powder**
> **3 tablespoons crunchy peanut butter**
> **2 teaspoons low salt soy sauce**
> **1 1/2 teaspoons chili sauce**
> **1 cup water**
> **2 tablespoons lemon juice**

tip from the chef

Marinating is an excellent way to ensure tenderness and add new flavor to meat. And it has the added bonus of keeping very lean meats juicy and tender. Try various combinations of aromatic spices and herbs with wine or low salt soy sauce –garlic, ginger, bay leaves, lemon rind, mustard, chili and rosemary are all excellent.

spiced prune and apricot compote

■□□ | Cooking time: 10 minutes - Preparation time: 10 minutes

ingredients

> **12 pitted prunes**
> **12 dried apricots**
> **1/2 cup raisins**
> **12 dried apple rings**
> **4 whole cloves**
> **1 small cinnamon stick**
> **1 teaspoon grated lemon rind**
> **2 teaspoons finely chopped candied ginger**
> **3/4 cup ginger wine**
> **3/4 cup water**

ginger dressing

> **1 cup diet fruit yogurt**
> **1 tablespoon honey**
> **1 tablespoon finely chopped candied ginger**

method

1. Place prunes, apricots, raisins, apple rings, cloves, cinnamon stick, lemon rind, ginger, ginger wine and water in a saucepan and bring slowly to the boil. Reduce heat and simmer, covered, for 10 minutes or until fruit is just tender.

2. Allow compote to cool and transfer to a serving dish. Cover and refrigerate for several hours or overnight.

3. To make dressing, blend together yogurt, honey and ginger. Just before serving, remove cloves and cinnamon stick from compote, top with dressing.

....
Serves 6

573 kilojoules/137 calories per serving

tip from the chef
Low fat yogurt is low in fat but not necessarily low in sugar. Diet yogurt is low in fat, artificially sweetened and has the least calories.

mini
fruit crumbles

■□□ | Cooking time: 20 minutes - Preparation time: 10 minutes

method

1. Place peaches, bananas and strawberries in a bowl and mix to combine (a). Divide fruit mixture between four 1 cup/250 ml/8 fl oz capacity ramekins.

2. To make topping, place muesli, honey and orange rind in a bowl (b) and mix to combine.

3. Sprinkle topping over fruit (c) and bake at 180°C/350°F/Gas 4 for 20 minutes or until topping is crisp and fruit is heated through.

....
Serves 4

887 kilojoules/212 calories per serving

ingredients

> 2 fresh peaches, peeled and chopped, or 440 g/14 oz unsweetened canned peaches, drained and chopped
> 2 bananas, chopped
> 250 g/8 oz strawberries, halved

muesli topping

> 1 cup/125 g/4 oz muesli
> 1 tablespoon honey
> 2 teaspoons finely grated orange rind

tip from the chef

Any combination of seasonal fruit can be used to make this tasty dessert. Serve with a spoonful of low fat natural yogurt or low fat fromage frais.

a

b

c

baked
strawberries and almonds

■□□ I Cooking time: 10 minutes - Preparation time: 10 minutes

ingredients
> **2 tablespoons slivered almonds**
> **¹/₂ cup apricot jam**
> **2 tablespoons Grand Marnier**
> **2 teaspoons sugar**
> **2 small boxes strawberries, hulled**

method
1. Place almonds on a baking tray and toast in moderate oven for 5 minutes.
2. Warm jam, Grand Marnier and sugar in small saucepan over low heat.
3. Arrange strawberries in a shallow ovenproof dish. Pour sieved jam mixture over strawberries.
4. Sprinkle almonds on top, bake in moderate oven for 5 minutes or until heated through.

Serves 4

1175 kilojoules/280 calories per serving

tip from the chef
Remember, fruit and vegetables come into the "eat most" category when you are trying to maintain a nutritious diet while restricting fat.

raspberry
and yogur

mousse

■□□ | Cooking time: 0 minute - Preparation time: 10 minutes

method

Place raspberries in a food processor or blender and process to make a purée (a). Press purée through a sieve to remove seeds. Stir in icing sugar.

Place ricotta cheese, yogurt, sugar, vanilla essence and lime or lemon juice in a food processor or blender (b) and process until smooth.

Divide mixture into two equal portions. Stir raspberry purée into one portion. Alternate spoonfuls of plain and raspberry mixtures in serving glasses (c) and swirl with a skewer. Refrigerate for at least 1 hour.

ingredients

> **300 g/10 oz fresh or frozen raspberries**
> **2 teaspoons icing sugar**
> **350 g/11¹/₂ oz low fat ricotta cheese**
> **1 cup/200 g/7 oz thick low fat natural yogurt**
> **2 tablespoons caster sugar**
> **2 teaspoons vanilla essence**
> **2 teaspoons lime or lemon juice**

....
Serves 6

647 kilojoules/155 calories per serving

tip from the chef

To make thick yogurt, line a sieve with a double thickness of muslin or absorbent kitchen paper and place over a bowl.

Place yogurt in sieve and set aside to drain for 2-3 hours at room temperature or overnight in the refrigerator.

a   b   c

lemon
ricotta puddings

■□□ | Cooking time: 25 minutes - Preparation time: 10 minutes

ingredients

- > **375 g/12¹/₂ oz low fat ricotta cheese**
- > **1 cup/200 g/7 oz low fat natural yogurt**
- > **1 egg**
- > **2 tablespoons lemon juice**
- > **2 teaspoons finely grated lemon rind**
- > **2 tablespoons sugar**
- > **1 teaspoon vanilla essence**

method

1. Place ricotta cheese, yogurt, egg, lemon juice, lemon rind, sugar and vanilla essence in a food processor or blender and process until smooth.

2. Divide mixture between four ³/₄ cup/ 185 ml/6 fl oz ramekins and bake at 180°C/350°F/Gas 4 for 25 minutes or until firm. Serve warm or cold.

....
Serves 4

895 kilojoules/214 calories per serving

tip from the chef
Fresh, full of flavor, rich in vitamin C and with only 134 kilojoules/32 calories per 100 g, lemon is great for weight watchers.

creamy cheesecake

a

■ ■ ☐ | Cooking time: 55 minutes - Preparation time: 15 minutes

method

1. To make base, combine cookie crumbs, hazelnuts and butter. Spread over the bottom of a lightly greased 22 cm/9 in springform tin (a) and set aside.
2. To make filling, place ricotta cheese, cottage cheese, semolina, buttermilk and egg yolks in a food processor or blender and process until smooth.
3. Beat egg whites (b) until soft peaks form. Add sugar a spoonful at a time, beating well after each addition until meringue is thick and glossy.
4. Fold cheese mixture into meringue (c), then lightly fold in lemon rind and sultanas.
5. Spoon mixture into prepared tin and bake at 180°C/350°F/Gas 4 for 50-55 minutes or until firm. Cool in tin.

Serves 8

1402 kilojoules/334 calories per serving

ingredients

base
> 1/2 cup cookie crumbs
> 1 tablespoon ground hazelnuts
> 1/4 cup butter, melted

filling
> 1 cup low fat ricotta cheese
> 1/2 cup cottage cheese
> 1 tablespoon fine semolina
> 2 tablespoons buttermilk
> 3 eggs, separated
> 3/4 cup superfine sugar
> 2 teaspoons grated lemon rind
> 3 tablespoons sultanas

tip from the chef

Instead of the usual cream cheese, we have used low fat ricotta cheese with cottage cheese and folded in beaten egg whites to create a smooth creamy texture. Our base has just enough butter to bind the cookie crumbs. Semolina thickens and sets the cake, reducing the need for another egg, so saving calories.

b

c

index